MAWLÂNA JALÂLEDDÎN-I RÛMÎ
THE LIFE, WORK AND THE MAWLAWÎ ORDER

Dr. Yakup Şafak

Konya / 2007

Editor
Mehmet Birekul

Authored by
Dr. Yakup Şafak

Translated by
Dr. M. Saim Kayadibi

Cover Design & Type Setting
Mümin Temizyürek

Redaction
Mawlâna Research Centre
University of Selcuk

Printing
Olgun Çelik Printing House

Konya / October 2007

ISBN: 978-605-000-003-0

Metropolitan Municipality of Konya
Cultural Series: 124

CONTENTS

FOREWORD / 4
THE LIFE OF MAWLÂNA, HIS ENVIRONMENT AND WORKS / 7
His Childhood And Education / 7
His Meeting With Shams Tabrizi / 10
After Shams / 11
His Family And Surroundings / 14
Works of Mawlâna / 16
MAWLÂNA'S THOUGHTS AND INFLUENCES / 21
Those Who Influenced Him And The Sources / 21
Thoughts / 22
Affects İn Turkish Culture And In The World / 30
THE WAY OF MAWLAWÎ ORDER, SEMÂ AND ELEGANCE EDUCATION / 33
REMEMBRANCES AND ADVICES FROM MAWLÂNA / 41
Mawlâna's Will / 47
Seven Advices / 47
Bibliography / 48

foreword
Tahir Akyürek
Mayor of Konya

The great philosopher Mawlâna Jalâleddîn-i Rùmî has been leading people almost every corner of the world through holding a mirror towards them. Mawlâna who is a spiritual light holding for human beings, had made distinctive and boundless tolerance a mile (mihenk) stone for his life.

Rúmí is a spiritual master before anything else. He has composed poetry but cannot be read as a mere poet. He has told stories but cannot be seen as a mere storyteller. Contrary to what some may think, he is not the guru of some new age religion movement. He is a murshíd and pír, a master who leads people to the path of spiritual refinement and realization. As borne out by the long history of the Mawlawí tradition and the recent popularity of Rúmí across the world, everyone finds something in him.

The present state of humanity is characterized by a deep crisis of spiritual impoverishment. The countless problems that surround us require urgent attention. And I know one thing for sure: we can overcome this impasse only by returning to Rúmí's eternal message about love and spiritual freedom.

In this respect, people who are having value chaos in the world, in order to be rightly comprehended and presented Mawlâna who is presenting the best messages in as much as a flower elegance the year of 2007 is holding a great importance.

Sometimes with hope, sometimes with yearning, sometimes with love, Mawlâna who is directing us towards seeking ourselves, all over the world need for his emphasises on tolerance, love, peace and hope.

I believe that declaring the year of 2007 is as the year of "Mawlâna Year" by Unesco, will have an opportunity to stay alive all these terms in agenda of the world and would be comprehended better.

THE LIFE OF MAWLÂNA, HIS ENVIRONMENT AND WORKS

His childhood and education

Mawlâna Jalâleddín Rûmî was born in 30 September 1207 in Balkh, where is located at the present Northern Afganistan. This city was, at that time, one of the main central city of Khorasan region. His original name is Mohammed. The name of "Mawlâna" means "Our Master or Excellency" was used as an esteemed title for great people and scholars. As to "Rûmî", it was used for those who are from Anatolia. Mawlâna belonged to a noble and a distinguished family. His mother was Mu'mine Khatun and his father was Bahaeddin Walad which was well known as the Sultan of Scholars (Sultan'ül-'Ulama'). His elder brother Alâaddin Mohammed and sister was Fâtıma Khatun.

According to a narration, that Bahaeddin Walad was at that time one of the caliphs of a great scholar and a Sufi leader Najm al-Din Kubra from Khorasan. The main reason of Bahaeddin Walad to decide him to migrate was his perception of the forthcoming Mongolian threat and a conflict, which was occurred between Bahaeddin Walad and Fakhreddin Râzî who was one of the famous philosopher and a scholars of Balkh because of Bahaeddin Walad's influential sermons and lectures on people, and attitudes of Sultan Mohammed Kharazmshah (d. 1220). He had left Balkh with his family members and a group of his followers. Fâtma Khatun stayed in Balkh due to his marriage. For the purpose of Pilgrimage they departed for the journey. During the long journey, they were respected everywhere they stoop up temporary quarters. When they met a great Sufi Farideddin Attar on their arrival at Nishabur, a little Jalâleddin was with them. Attar had gifted one of his copy of Asrarnâme to Jalâleddin and said to Bahaeddin Walad about Jalâleddin "Take care of this child and give him high respect for him, not very long time you will see that he will set fire onto the heart of the lovers in this world."

The convoy stopped by Dimishq (Sham) after duty of pilgrimage, after a while they travelled towards Erzincan. On the request of administrators those who give high respects to them, for a while, they spent sometimes in Akshehir Erzincan. After travelling around Anatolia for sometimes, they settled down in Lârende, which is now Karaman. Jalaleddin married Gawhar Khatun, the daughter of Khaja Lala al Samarqandi who left Balkh together with Jalâleddin's family, when he was about eighteen year old, in Lârende. They had two sons, Bahâeddin Mohammed (Sultan Walad) and Alâaddin Mohammed. The family had stayed in Lârende for seven years. Mawlâna's mother Mu'mine khatun and his eldest brother Alâaddin died and were buried here during the stay.

Bahâeddin Walad and along with his family and friends, with an invitation of an estimable and a just ruler Sultan Alâaddin Keykubad I. moved from Karaman to Konya in 1229.

The Sultan and his people met them on the way with high respect, and provided for them Palaca to stay in comfortably. Despite of the Sultan's invitation to the Palace, Bahâeddin Walad refused his invitation kindly preferred staying in the madrasah. Konya was the capital of Anatolian Seljuks where especially with the interests, respects and encouragements of rulers, so many scholars, Sufis, artists and intellectuals preferred to move in and it is a place where people took refuge from the Mongolian attacks at that time. When Bahâeddin Walad died he was 80 years of age, the people wanted Jalâleddin should take his father's place. However, after a short while Sayyid Burhâneddin Mukaggig-i Tirmizî, a caliph of Bahâeddin

Walad came to Konya. Jalâleddin's fist teacher (murshid) was his father, Sultânü'l-Ulemâ (Bahâeddin Walad). His father's disciple Sayyid Burhâneddin took over the responsibility for his spiritual training as he arrived at high rank of external knowledge. Mawlâna, too, left himself to the guidance of Sayyid Burhâneddin and stayed under his supervision. His attitude had changed and by the request of his master, he went to Halab and Damascus, important education centres at that time, in order to complete his education. He returned back to Anatolia after a long time of education. He continued ascetic training by the wish of his teacher (murshid). Finally, having passed this long period with self-purification and meditations his heard finally opened to divine secrets, turned his attention to the world outside. At the end of the spiritual training Sayyid Burhâneddin with the following words that Mawlâna's training had finished successfully and he had been charged with spiritual guidance (murshid) "You were a unique in all rational and transmitted (naqli) knowledge; however, now you became a favourite for saints and prophets on the way of arriving at the spiritual secrets and realities."

A great scholar and a sufi Sayyid Burhâneddin who is known as Sayyid-i Sırdan (master of secrets) died in 1242 in Kayseri. Mawlâna, after this time, started to enlighten people and teach religious knowledge. Especially in jurisprudence and hadíth he arrived at high rank of knowledge; at the state of qadi who gives religious rulings. According to a narration he has hundreds of students and followers, his fame spread out everywhere. He was influenced by his father and his teacher Sayyid Burhâneddin, took modesty viewpoints from both side. Due to this, while he was engaged with education, on the other side he was busy with Gazali's Sufi principles which were combined by the religious rulings.

HIS MEETING WITH SHAMS TABRIZI

While days were passing as usual, a strange look person, a traveller derwish named Shams Tabrizi came to Konya. When he met Mawlâna, he left extraordinary strange effect on him. Probably Mawlâna had seen him either in Halab or in Dimishq (Sham). There are different narrations on Mawlâna's meeting with Shams. However, the obvious one is that Mawlâna had changed suddenly when he saw Shams. Mawlâna who was wishing to go forward in the spiritual way and following spiritual men, finally he found what he was wishing within the wise man. As he invited him with showing respect and request in his home, he has been spending all his time with him but others. He had cut off sermon, minbar and lecturing at the madrasah (university). After being together for a long time, months and months, Mawlâna had changed his way. He had worn his sufi cardigan and was telling poems in the atmosphere of love, ecstasy, high spirits and exuberance. He had started whirling (semâ) despite he did not give any attention when he was following his father and Sayyid Burhâneddin's footstep before. Reed flute (ney) and rebab tunes were echoed in his assembly.

As Mawlâna, he who is a scholar who had been a beloved one for the people, was hunted by Shams, he who is a person who had been a saucy and a far away from wisdom and even he is not known who is he? Also disappearing, being with Shams for months, spending everything what he owned for the sake of his way, leaving the lecturing ruling, sermon and appearing with ecstasy, those who are around Mawlâna assumed a hostile attitude against Shams, even caused them to call hostile him "magician". Shams suddenly disappeared due to the people's attitudes and words. Those who were expecting that Mawlâna would return his old nature, after

16 months being together when Shams left, were actually deceived. While he was in a miserable and sorrowful situation, he was insisting on that Shams has to be found, telling poems and could not calm down. Finally, after 15 months one day he heard a news that he is in Dimishq, he sent his son Sultan Walad with his some relatives to Dimishq to excuse him and to invite him to Konya.

Mawlâna became extraordinary happy due to Shams' agitated feelings, which made him to come Konya. His followers excused him. He, too, forgave them. Whirling assembly began to be organized. Mawlâna and Shams were being invited for every days by someone who has ability. However, this situation did not last longer. When Mawlâna spent couple of times with Shams, the people began gossiping again against Shams. Mawlâna's second son Alâaddin Çelebi was also involved into the second instigation, which is stronger then the first one. A group of Mawlâna's followers and some relatives decided to kill Shams and killed him secretly, they hided his dead body or according to a different narration, he had left Konya in 1242 and never heard anything about him any more.

His sudden disappearance stupefied Mawlâna. Day and night he is telling poems, whirling, could not calm he down even for a second he never became in peace and quite. There you are, most of the poems in Dîvân-ı Kebîr which is contained about 40 thousand couplets, were formed while he was within the state of mind. It is obvious that such state of mind should not be expressed by any language other then poem and music.

AFTER SHAMS

Mawlâna's state of mind, after meeting with Shams, made angry

MAWLÂNA JALÂLEDDÎN-I RÛMÎ

some scholars and judges. They have been telling that what they have been doing was against the religion. Mawlâna who was hurt by all of them, even he went to Dimishq for twice to search Shams, as he could not find his footprint, returned back to Konya. After this return in 1250, Mawlâna gradually regains his consciousness. Finally, he "sun" raised within his existence and found him within.

Jalâleddin Mohammed who was educated by under the control of a skilful and an influential father, a valuable shaykh as a great scholar, judge and a Sufi, towards his mature life, a unique example in the history, he was before the people as Mawlâna who was a person that is inflamed by a man of love. His extraordinary intellect and a unique personality, an example education which he had, were constructed on great soul with his strong and principle knowledge, vast feelings and uninterrupted love. These characteristics of him were reflecting on the people as great love, wide range of tolerance and a vast worldly vision.

His trustworthiness, realistic, not interesting in worldly matters, self confidence, to have struggle soul, characteristics of ready response, being open minded for dialogue to everybody, valuable ideas, original and evoke admiration comments and wide horizon, he had great approval by the people. From statesmen to artists, tradesmen, even non-Muslims, he gained love and respect of wide range of people; he converted the attitudes and sayings, which were against him, to his favour. Of course there was an important role of Seljukis' tolerant administration.

Mawlâna, he who was living on some money which was provided by the government for his ruling (fatwa) duty, from this time, even more he became busy with guiding Sufis and wise people and showing the way to the people. He obtained as caliph and friend of him jewellers Salâhaddin who is one of the followers of Sayyid Burhâneddin. Despite, some of the people around Mawlâna was uncomfortable about uneducated person Salâhaddin to be appointed for this post, Mawlâna continued his relationship with Salâhaddin who was unconditionally devoted himself; even he married his son Sultan Walad with his daughter Fâtıma Khatun. Salâhaddîn-i Zerkûb, after ten years being a very close friendship, was becoming sick died in 1258. Mawlâna was highly effected by this again and wrote some poems. In any case, within pain of separateness never vanished from him and never became state of calm and comfort. Even though he continued his life struggle and always had been in the society.

Chalabi Hüsâmeddin became his caliph and confidant after Salâhaddin's death. He who is known as Ahi Türkoğlu was knowledgeable and a wise man. Chalabi Hüsâmeddin, he who is devoted himself with love and respect to Mawlâna, had requested from him to write a book which explain the truth of Sufism for derwishes. He then took out a piece of paper from his turban that was written on the first eighteen couplets of Mathnawí and gave them Chalabi Hüsâmeddin; he told him that he would tell if he accepts to write. Mawlâna had passed his 10 or 15 year of his life writing the Mathnawí. Every opportunity he was telling poems and Chalabi Hüsâmeddin was writing. There for, the great six volumes, which it consists of about 26 thousand couplets, came into existence. Mawlâna was attaching great importance Mathnawí, every possible time he expresses his gratitude to Chalabi Hüsâmeddin. He was expressing the mission of Mathnawí as: "After us the Mathnawí will have the post for guidance, will show for those who are looking for, will control them and lead them for the truth."

MAWLÂNA JALÂLEDDÎN-I RÛMÎ

After the great ruler Alâaddin Keykubad, system of the state and the unity began to be spoiled, peace and comfort in the society began to get lost in Seljuks. In such atmosphere, existence of Mawlâna and his ideas became a source of comfort and a shelter. Of course this matter has role too, in the respect and love which was shown him by every side of the society. Mawlâna Jalâleddin Rumi's body, he who all of his life was passed through love, hardship and struggle, was tired. At the end of his life his days were passing with illnesses. Finally he came together with his eternal lover at the sunset on Sunday in 17 December 1273. Mawlawís have called this night "Shab-i Arûs" which is wedding night and they commemorate this extraordinary night with variety of celebrations for centuries. His funeral was sent to eternal journey participating with every body, which consists of young and old even non-Muslim people.

HIS FAMILY AND SURROUNDINGS

We have already mentioned that Mawlâna has got two sons whose mother is Gawhar Khatun. Bahâeddin (Sultan Walad) who is the eldest of them, sincerely obeyed to his father and always followed his footsteps. His other son, Alâaddin had left his family because of his involvement in the case of murder of Shams and had died in 1262.

After death of his first wife, Gawhar Khatun, Mawlâna married Kirâ Khatun, who is a widow. He had two children a girl Malika and a boy Amir Âlim from the second wife. Amir Âlim had spent his life for the servant of government and Malika Khatun married a trader Shahâbeddin. Amir Âlim deceased in 1277 and Malika Khatun in 1292.

Mawlâna had contact with every individuals of the society in Konya in which it is a capital of Anatolian Seljuks and a shelter for the distinguished people of the time. Surroundings of him mainly consisted of tradesmen, craftsmen and people of the society. Besides this, he was in good relationships with statesmen, scholars, Sufis, artists and distinguished people of the society.

Seljuki rulers were having deep respect to him. Mawlâna, in his life time had seen the governance of I. Alâaddin Keykubad (1219-1237), II. Gıyâseddin Keyhusrev (1237-1246), II. İzzeddin Keykâvus (1246-1257 by himself or together), II. Alâaddin Keykubad (1248-1257 together), IV. Kılıç Arslan (1248-1265 by himself or together) and III. Gıyâseddin Keyhusrev (1265-1282). We should mention amongst them especially relationship of I. Alâaddin Keykubad, II. İzzeddin Keykâvus and IV. Kılıç Arslan with him.

As it is known that at the period when Mawlâna and his family moved to Konya, the sovereignty has been living in a bright period especially because of I. Alâaddin who was famous for his justice and goodness. At that time, Anatolia was a place of peace and comfort. In Anatolia, Those who migrated because of Mongolian invasion and great scholars, Sufis, statesmen, artists, grew up in here, the people had lived in a safe and comfort life even the sovereignty did not last longer.

Some of the famous scholars and Sufis who were in Konya at the era of Mawlâna are: Muhyiddin Ibnu'l-Arabî, Kutbeddîn-i Shîrâzî, Najmaddîn-i Dâye, Awhaduddîn-i Kirmânî, Sadraddîn-i Konewî, Qadi Sirâjaddîn-i Urmavî, Fahreddîn-i Irâqî. Yunus Amra and Haji Baktash-i Wali also a great Sufi who lived at the century of Mavlâna.

MAWLÂNA JALÂLEDDÎN-I RÛMÎ

WORKS OF MAWLÂNA

One of the greatest personality of our cultural and literature history Mawlâna Jalâleddin Rûmî (1207-1273), had left for the humanity at the end of his life that passed through exuberant of love and pain of separation, expressed the most sincere emotions of a lover soul, greatly indicated Sufi teachings the following works which contains prose and poetry writings.

Dîvân-ı Kebîr: means great Dîvân. The great work, which contains gazels, tarkib-i bend and rubâis, was organized according to the meter of poems that was contained by 21 dîvâns and rubâis which is about 40 thousand couplets.

After meeting Shams-i Tabrîzî, Mawlâna who he dived into Love Ocean, turned towards poem and music, which is a sole device naturally as to respond to a lover soul's emotions; started whirling through Shams' encouragement. Mawlâna after this time at the period of his life as if he acquired poem, music, whirling as his friends on the spiritual journey; his enthusiasm, exuberance, happiness, sadness, he always expressed them through these tools, looked for peace and comfort through them. We know that he said the most of the gazels for the sake of Shams-i Tebrîzî's disappearance. Many times the exuberant poetry what he said during the whirling, kept by his lovers and these were organized according to arùz meters. The scientific text of the work had been published by an esteemed scholar Iranian Bedîuzzaman Furûzanfer. It was translated into Turkish by Abdulbâki Golpinarli.

Mathnawî, is a great work, which almost includes twenty-six thousand couplets in six volumes, informing us stories which were developed through religious, philosophy, etiquette and social aspects. For centuries this work, which has been a main source kneading our culture, and our sense and thought world, was known by its literal description as much as containing its inner thought. As the Mathnawî is considered "Essence of Qur'an", almost every kind of theme that concerns the society took part in it. Mawlâna presented to readers every kind of topics from religious and etiquette conducts to government administrations, from work lives to health, from shopping to conflicts, from philosophy and divinity to psychological and sociological analysis, from the creation of the universe to formation of atoms in his great work through a beautiful expressions, with an incomparable imitations and examples which were supported by the most effective and persuasive evidences; analyzing the issues through literal method in length and breath rather fluently and fascinating way.

This great book has been read by woman-man, young-old, and every kind of people for centuries, it was explained by Mathnawîkhan to either followers of the tarîqat (dervish order) or people, it was translated and interpreted by many scholars and Sufis, many selections were made from itself, classified by theme, prepared its dictionaries, become an inspiration to works, thoughts, art and literature works. At the period of Ottoman Surûrî (d. 1562), Sham'î (d. 1600 after), Ankaravî (d. 1631), Yusuf Dede (d. 1669), Nahîfî (d. 1738), Shakir Mehmed (d. 1836), Mehmed Murad (d. 1847) became successful in translation or interpretation of whole Mathnawî. Regarding some part of Mathnawî –especially the first volume- was written many works containing its translation and interpretation.

Scientifically Mathnawî's Persian text first was considered by English Oriental Nicholson during the years of 1925-1940, again by the same person it was interpreted and translated into English. Especially Tâhirü'l-Mawlawî, Walad Izbudak and Abdulbâki Golpinarli should

MAWLÂNA JALÂLEDDÎN-I RÛMÎ

be mentioned as to those who are amongst the people who interpreted and translated Mathnawî. Recent years, deceased Shafik Can had valuable works upon Mathnawî.

Fîhi Mâ Fîh: it means the things are in it or what ever in it is it. It is a prose work, which contains Mawlâna's lectures and mostly summarised stories in Mathnawî. It becomes an important work which reflects whether his life or different cases in his time, thought and beliefs.

Majâlis-i Sab'a which means seven assembly. It contains Mawlâna's speeches and advices in mosques. It is formed in seven parts.

Maktûbât It is the collection of Mawlâna's letters to statesmen, to the important and prominent personalities of his time. It is important especially for the consideration of Seljuks history. (These three prone work's Persian texts were published and translated into Turkish of our time.)

MAWLÂNA'S THOUGHTS AND INFLUENCES

THOSE WHO INFLUENCED HIM AND THE SOURCES

The first name comes across to the mind among those who influenced Mawlâna is his father Bahâeddin Walad who is such a great scholar and a Sufi who deserved to be called "Sultânü'l-'Ulemâ" and after his death was his caliph Sayyid Burhâneddin Muhaqqıq-ı Tirmizî. Upon Mawlâna, especially before Shams, one of the influential personalities with their work was Imâm-ı Gazâlî. An Iranian esteemed scholar Jalâl Hümâyî expressed this influence saying, "Mawlâna, before became Mawlâna he was Gazâlî". There are two Iranian influential great Sufi poets upon Mawlâna. These are Hakîm Sanâî and Farîdüddîn-i Attâr. Besides these, such poets Hâkânî, Nizâmî, Anwarî's traces are seen in Mawlâna's works especially in Dîvân-ı Kebîr; on the other hand, important personalities of Arab literature, such as Imru'l-Qays, Ka'b bin Zuheyr and in the period of ignorant; Mutanabbî, Abû Tammâm, Abu'l-Alâ al-Maarrî those who lived in the period of Islam, their names and poems took part on the list. Abdulbâki Golpinarli who wrote at the monograph saying that Mawlâna comprehended many cultures before him completely, the Greek- Iran mythology, profession of Batlamius, Egypt and Indian cultures, Interpretation of Qur'an, Hadith, Islamic Theology, Logic (Mantiq) and classical knowledge, especially Sufism. Of course, in some old encyclopaedic sources, he is mentioned as famous Hanafi scholars among them. The great scholar Badîuzzaman Furûzanfar who made successful work that was the most comprehensive and valuable works upon Mawlâna's life and works, the details, which enlightens these themes, can be found in his works. In this context, it should be expressed the influence and importance of Shams-i Tabrîzî lately played a turning point in Mawlâna's life. Mawlâna Jalâleddin Rûmî had entered the way of divine love and ecstasy through the great wise man, through his spark he became fire and finely became Mawlâna.

Mawlâna's all works, especially if his Mathnawî, which is a "cultural world", is investigated, it is seen that the peoples those who were attributed and pointed as examples by Mawlâna and the works and themes are not different than a simple Sufi's. Therefore, we are able to say that his difference than others is the style, the way of uttering. His explanations are so much effective, persuasive and original. Even this is the same for many complicated cases which tired Islamic world for centuries.

THOUGHTS

It is known that Sufism, which is a kind of interpretation and practise of Islam, has near and far objective. Its near objective is to educate people who will be good, etiquette, pure and having a strong personality; far objective is to give respond to the main issues and problems which has been kept busy the humanity since the day of human being existence, that is to say that to convey belongings to the Right and truth. To arrive at these objectives, Mawlâna who he is one of the people among those who appropriated himself to the way of divine love, he express this reality with the following sayings: "How you could arrive at such an unreachable stage of the Muhammad (pbuh) pass through without Love Burâq and the guidance of Gabriel (perfect guidance)?" (DK.4/278); "The Divine Love is the Sun of perfection: the (Divine) command is its light, the creatures are as shadows." (Mathnawî. 6/983). As it was indicated in a Hadíth-i Qudsí "I was a Hidden Treasure and loved to be known. Therefore I created the Creation that I might be known". The main reason and fundamental power of the Creation is Self Love "aşk-ı zâtî" which means the Supreme Authority God's Self

Love and Liking Himself. In that respect "It is the fire of Love that is in the reed, it is the fervour of Love that is in the wine." (Math. 1/10) "If Love were not be, the world would be frozen." (Math.5/3854) "The love of Him from whose love all the prophets gained power and glory. (Math.1/220) Our Prophet's way is a way of love. (Genc.,Rub.49) It is a feeling that this love surrounds lover's whole life, moment and conceit and always produces conscious of slavery and eagerness for worshiping.

Mawlâna is one of the unique representatives of the love of Allah in the world. His book Dîwân-ı Kabîr, which consists of poems, is generally full of begs and praise to the past and future eternal Love. However, the poems in here rather appear to express the difficulties of love and yearnings, to express his sorrows: praise the Love sometimes, reproach sometimes and beg that would be suitable to the classical poem's rhetoric. In contrast this, direct expression is obvious in Mathnawî. Therefore, the best examples of entreating to God can be possible to find too there.

The most mentioned and pointed example people in Mathnawî are of course prophets and saints. Mawlâna expresses them as they are leader of having the same mission walking towards the right truth and God. He says: "Every prophet and every saint has a way of religious doctrine and practice (profession and methods) but it leads to God all the ways are really one." (1/3086). In his expression "He (such a person) is one that acquaints (you) with things hidden, like the Prophet who has seen what the people of this world have not seen." (3/2960), "The prophets have conferred a great obligation (on us), because they have made us aware of the end." (6/3770), Who should be more persuasive in counselling and sweeter-tongued than the prophets, whose words made an impression (even) on stones? (5/1534), (The shadow mentioned in the words) How He (God) extended the shadow is the form of the saints, which guides to the light of the Divine Sun. Do not go in this valley without this guide; say, like Khalíl (Abraham), "I love not them that set," (1/425-426). He (God) brought the saints on to the earth, in order that He might make them a mercy to (all) created beings. (3/1804) He has died to self and become living through the Lord: hence, the mysteries of God are on his lips. (3/3364)

In this context, he mentions the extraordinary place of our beloved Prophet for some reason: expresses always his incomparable mission in guidance; remembers him with the best imitations, with the most sincere expressions; "the Prophet Mohammed's (pbuh) light was divided into millions parts and covered throughout the two worlds." "Fresh destiny friend, our work is to sacrifice our soul; the head of the caravan is Mustafa (pbuh) who is proud of by the world. Even the moon was split when it saw the moon face; it arrived at the good fortune due to obeying him." (DK. 3/189,4/358) "He is the intercessor in this world and in yonder world—in this world (for guidance) to the (true) religion, and yonder (for entrance) to Paradise. In this world he says, "Do You show unto them the Way, and in yonder world he says, "Do You show unto them the Moon. By his breath (powerful intercession) both the Gates were opened: in both worlds his prayer is answered. He has become the Seal (of the prophets) for this reason that there never was any one like him in munificence nor ever shall be." (Math.6/167-71) "Look at the Religion of Muhammed (pbuh), has passed 650 years after the migration it still stand strong... how strong structure it is! You cant see anything about Abu Lahab and those who look like him. But only their stories have been told for drawing a lesson. (DK.3/97). Anyhow, he with this couplet determined his devotion to the Qur'an and the Prophet (pbuh):

"I am the servant of the Qur'an as long as I have life. I am the dust on the path of Muhammed (pbuh), the Chosen one. If anyone quotes anything except this from my sayings, I am quit of him and outraged by these words. (R.No: 1052).

At the beginning of Mathnawî, it starts with "Listen to the reed how it tells a tale, complaining of separations?", human beings departed from its original hometown which is the world of soul, from its beloved and from its friends that was dramatically symbolised with Ney (reed). Becoming perfect kneaded with pain and sorrows in this foreign land, maturated through divinely be able to arrive at his origin which means source of the eternal values. Man always struggling with its self, involving every part of the society, having pain, be able to develop; purified from sediments like gold and silver. However, man stands against its pain and sorrows just to spite love and ambition; he should avoid pains, which occurred by either himself or the same kind/race or life stipulations, through "love emerald". On the other hand, "he who hasn't got portion of greatness" should have material subsistence melted; establish the sovereignty of the soul. It is praised to have success of struggling without segregating himself from the society, personal and social realities.

As it is indicated in the exalted Book Qur'an, the real satisfaction in man is something related to soul. The soul is in fact fall in love with its origin. Mawlâna's living divine love and his dynamic perspective without separating himself from the reality of life had infected too his prays and method towards God. Mawlâna who mentions that atoms and stars are moving always and turning around, he wanted to explore the great realty through the concept of semâ (whirling) which is one of the principles of his way.

MAWLÂNA JALÂLEDDÎN-I RÛMÎ

According to Mawlâna happiness is something that giving up selfless and turning towards God, slipping off from self-desires and narrow patterns of limited intellect to be free and look for the reality: "O son, burst your chains and be free! How long will you be a bondsman to silver and gold?" (Math.1/19) "If there is my ayran bowl in front of me, I swear God I do not think of anybody's honey bowl. Even if death rubbed my ear with poverty, I never exchange freedom for slavery." (R.No: 935) what Mawlâna said, he is a perfect freedom lover. According to him, real freedom comes from real guidance and prophets. Believers had become free by owing to Prophets.

Great thinker indicates that intellect, which is not nourished by its origin, will not be avoided from to be the same as those who describe elephant in dark. Because he is advising as "Do not make sensuality your vizier; even if you have intellect, associate and consult with another intellect; make the Universal Intellect your vizier." Mawlâna in another saying, he describes body as a ruins. However, man as his nature wants to be contended with available and to protect it. He is afraid of moving away to new horizons and new climates. Whereas there is a treasure under the ruins, that he supposed it a palace. If he is able to demolish the house, for from one treasure in hand it is possible to build a thousand houses and of course palaces are deserving to host Kings." (Math.4/2540 etc.)

In this perspective, the main basis of wide tolerance and indulgence which was shown to human beings by Mawlâna and like many Sufis, there is trust on essence and hope that they hold. As like Yunus Emre says "We love all the creation for the sake of the Creator.", Mawlâna's saying is identical "Which seed did not grow when it is planted? Why don't you think the same for men?

(DK.3/169). Even if there are his naughty and unbearable attitudes, he carries the deposit of beloved that is sacrificed how many souls for men. Otherwise, Mawlâna should not avoid telling his heavy criticism that you can not find anywhere else, when an occasion appears, to those who are uneducated, thoughtless and irresponsible. As he says, "To show mercy to thieves and any sinister-handed (noxious) person is to inflict blows and have no mercy on the weak." (Math.6/4261). One of the distinguished personalities of him is biting reality. Struggle of those who see and show Mawlâna single sided towards their own desires must be obliged to come to naught towards this obvious reality.

Limitless and ebullient love of Mawlâna is a power, which unites, and combines individuals around the same values and melting them in the same crucible that was reflected to the society as love, tolerance, brotherhood and solidarity. "By love bitter things become sweet; by love pieces of copper become golden; By love dregs become clear; by love pains become healing; By love the dead is made living; by love the king is made a slave. (Math.2/1529-30) "Whoever gets on well with his lover, never be without lover; he who gets on well with customer, never be bankrupted; the moon remained as bright, because it was not frightened; rose too obtained the smell because suited itself with thorn." (R.No: 211) The great thinker who says "In my religion one of my foot is fixed, but with the other I roam the seventy-two nations." Regarding this saying of Mawlâna he gave appreciation to human beings and respected them regardless of being any religion, nation, colour, man-woman, reach-poor if you are a human being then you share a basic commonality with the others. Boundless compassion, appreciating man, yearning to the peaceful and happy live, briefly, thoughts are described as "humanism", of course has taken its source from Islam.

Mawlâna who embraced Islam with a deep soul, excitement and art, with the inspiration, which he had from his belief, he was full of deep sympathy, respect and tolerance to everybody and all kinds of creations. The source of universality in his personality, in his works and in his influential power, of course should be searched in here. Every single word, which is uttered from Mawlâna's mouth, and behaviour is full of unity, brotherhood messages. His calling is to the all people and humankind. "O friends, friends! Do not separated. Throw loophole desires from you. Since you are one, do not sing a duality song. The King of loyalty is ordering; do not be disloyal! (R.No: 642). The world which is on they way to be a little village or a little town, with the concept of globalisation, they such need of unity and peace call of Mawlâna. However, to obtain the unity, man always must turn towards his Creator and desires needs from Him. "Desire wealth from Him, not from treasure and possessions: desire aid from Him, not from paternal and maternal uncles." (Math.5/1497)

Mawlâna, assurance of brotherhood and solidarity in the society, while insistently emphasising the role of belief and spiritual dynamics, in this context, he reminds that the main determiner is love and solidarity of feelings: "Those who share the same feelings can understand each other, not those are speaking the same language." (Math. 2/3681) "There is a passage heart to heart; brotherhood and enmity pass through this hidden way." "If a believer be a mirror of other believer, nobody can see other's faults." (DK.6/209). While he was against injustice and despotism, "The iniquity of evildoers is a dark well, O you who from iniquity are digging a well (for others), you are making a snare for yourself." (Math. 1/1309) on the other hand, "The waves of peace dash against each other and root up hatreds from (men's) breasts. In other form do the waves of war turn (men's) loves upside down (confound and destroy them)." (Math.1/2578) with these words he emphasis on goodwill and peace which is difficult and virtuous, not hatred and revenge which is easy and simple.

According to him, things that mature man is either sufferings of individual life or life struggles. Therefore, "Go and search for yourself sorrow, find sorrow; choose sorrow from pains! Because, there is no way to live other than this. Do not be upset you destiny became your fortune. Only if you don't have sorrow then show unhappiness. (R.No: 1177) Fighting suits for man for both worlds. It is needed to have sorrow from both stone and coral. A man either live as a man dressed or to bear thousand kind of shames." (R.No: 1171) It can be said that constant movement in the way of God, continues development and progress is His infallible characters. "Yesterday has gone, the day before yesterday is past, day is today." (R.No: 142) Emphasising Mawlâna on innovation and being on formation every moment is because of this. This following quatrain beautifully explains his thoughts. "Migrating everyday from somewhere is how good! Settling everyday somewhere is how beautiful! How nice! to flow without freezing and muddying. My darling has gone away with yesterday, whatever something to be said regarding yesterday. New things should be said now!" (A.Gölpınarlı, Mevlâna Celâleddin, p.297)

Despite of today modern life's opportunities given to the people, those who are not satisfied with provision of biological needs, not to accept being a simple consumption tools in merciless competitions, even more seek deep meaning of the life and want to fill spiritual blank in their life, rushing and rushing running towards Mawlâna's ideas that embrace entire human beings, wide love and tolerance; coming to his spiritual presence; participating with their hearts to peacefully turning whirling dervishes aimed to clean their souls. The love and interests which contains millions is of course a trace of sincerity, warmth, those who are connected through their hearts; these are the result of high values that we have.

AFFECTS IN TURKISH CULTURE AND IN THE WORLD

Mawlâna Jalâleddín Rûmî, during his life and after his death influenced so many people and communities, is a great Islamic philosopher and a Sufi. Whether in the geography of Islam or other part of the world, there is a very little people who drew attention, respect and love. Mawlâna who is a symbol of being love of Allah, love of the Prophet and tolerance and respect to people; model of unity and cooperation, today he is our interpreter of thoughts and feelings, voice of us that spread out from Konya to the world.

Mawlâna Jalâleddín Rûmî, with the saying of one of our famous thinkers Hilmi Ziya Ülken, is "one of the greatest personalities of our thousand years cultural history. He is not only a great poet, founder of a dervish order, a deep Sufi, a wise scholar, but also he is a great soul and a movement leader who ensured a great unity and combination among the ethnic components in Anatolian culture. (Hilmi Yücebaş, Edebiyatımızda Mevlâna, İst., 1959, s. 10.) In that the conscious unity, he aimed to embody the love of Allah and the Prophet into the hearts, advocated Islam to be practised in the context of sincerity and love.

From Mawlaví dervish convents that was established on the thoughts of him, great poets artists were grown, for centuries. This dervish convent (taríqat), which was taken its fame for delicacy, either the notables or the wide range of the society had shown their respects. Dervish convents have been playing a central role of fine-art academies for centuries. As in the Turkish literature, in the field of Turkish music, in the variety of fields of fine-arts too, can be often met Mawlawí poets such as Itrî, İsmail Dede Efendi, Zekâî Dede, master of music and many other Artists in many other fields. Many statesmen and famous people has joined to this tarîqat or had respect to Mawlawí tarîqat. So many poets, from Sultan Ahmed who wrote poems under the pseudonym Bahtî to Nâbî, from Nef'î' to Gâlib', from Yahya Kemal to Arif Nihad Asya wrote such beautiful poems praising Mawlâna.

Influence of Mawlâna, of course, was not confined to Anatolia only, but especially Iran and Indian continent, his influence had great effect; so many scholars, Sufis and literalists were interested in his works, wrote valuable explanations. At the East and the West today an extraordinary interest to him and to his work was increasing. Nowadays both in the country and the abroad, researches regarding Mawlâna and his works dramatically were increasing. The Mathnawí has already translated into main languages and this activities are continuing. Especially those who got jammed into the narrow matrix of material are researching a spiritual peace and tranquil, in the search of peaceful life that would make their life meaningful had arrived at enormous numbers in the Western people. Today the WebPages that contain the words of "Mawlâna" and "Rûmî" have reached to hundreds and thousands, the works of Mawlâna have taken place in the most wanted books in USA for years. His works were read in many occasions and used for psychotherapy methods, composed his poems, on the name of him, so many associations were established, and became a theme for cultural activities, it would be understood the level of context that reached. Through the recommendation of UNESCO, the 800th birthday anniversary, has taken part in the year of 2007 that is celebrated all over the world as the year of Mawlâna Jalâleddín Rûmî, taking into consideration of Semá as cultural heritage lists of the world that would be protected is also to show respect and love towards him.

THE WAY OF MAWLAVÎ ORDER, SEMÂ AND ELEGANCE EDUCATION

After the decease of Mawlâna Jalâleddín Rûmî who played great role as his boundless thoughts as, the unity of Anatolia and settling there, establishment of Turkish literature, Chalabi Hüsâmeddin had proposed him to take the post of his father, however, he did not accepted it and he wanted Chalabi Hüsâmeddin to stay in his father's post. When Chalabi Hüsâmeddin died in 1284, Mawlâna's loyal son Sultan Walad had ascended the post. Sultan Walad had represented properly this post for a long time and he systematised the Mawlaví understanding as a proper dervish order (sect). When he died in 1312, this post had been undertaken by his son Ulu Ârif Chalabi. After that, Pír Âdíl Chalabi (d.1461) had developed and rearranged the rules, manners (âdâb) and conditions of the dervish order (sect). Since Sultan Walad, the Mawlawí sect always has been represented by someone who is called Chalabi whose lineage goes back to Mawlâna.

Mawlawí sect, which is organized at first around Konya, later other cities, it is spread out especially at the period of emporium from Egypt until the central Austria because of giving attention of Ottoman Sultans to high mannered, modest and cultured sect. Mawlawí dervish convents were established around there and Mawlawí rituals were performed, Mawlawí semâ (whirling), its music were interested well-known throughout the three continents. (N.S.Banarlı, RTET, İst., 1971, I, 293.)

Mawlawí convents usually were located in a big garden out of the city. One side of the convent there is a cemetery (hâmûşhâne) and on the other side, there is a harem lodge where the family of shaykh would be able to stay in. Main building of Mawlawí convent consists of mosque, whirling hall (semâhane), and a tomb. Founder of the convent and

MAWLÂNA JALÂLEDDÎN-I RÛMÎ

great shaykhs were buried in the tomb. Out side there are matbah-ı şerif (kitchen), dervish cells, entrance, selâmlık and also a library, courtyard, fountains, toilet, washing room etc. All the Mawlawí convents are connected to the Main convent (Mevlâna Âsitâne) where is located in Konya that seems to be centrally administered. (Âsitâne is somewhere which chille (forty days seclusion) is experienced which means that Mawlawí convents where dedes were educated in; the other small Mawlawí convents were called zâviye). More than hundred Mawlawí convents, in Ottoman period, were connected with Chalebi Efendi who was at the head of Konya Convent (Dergâhı).

Postnishes (sheikh) were appointed from the centre (Konya Mawlawí Âsitânesine). Newniyâz someone who is applying for dervishhood, at first educated in the Matbakh-ı Sharif. The candidate was seat on the Saka post, then if the candidate was accepted, after three days he pronounces and is accepted to fulfil 1001 days chille (seclusion). Besides the manner and conditions of Mawlawi sect, semâ (whirling) were exercised in Matbakh (kitchen). Writing-reading were thought and literature, art, and handcraft for those who are talented were thought for Suffering "soul"s. Not only Mawlána's works but also religious lessons were taught there too. On the other hand, books about the manner of tarâkat (sect) and its history were studied. Love, wisdom and service, which is the main principles of tarîkat (sect) education, were practiced there.

After Chalabi Efendi, in Konya Âsitane, main teachers (zâbitan) were in sequence as follows: Head of the dervishes (ser-tarîk-Tarîkatçi), head of the cook (ser-tabbâh), guard of the tomb of Mawlâna, guard of the tomb of Shams, guard of the tomb Âteshbâz, head of the flute player, head of the drum player. In addition to that stoker (Kazancı) and middleman (Meydancı) dedes have a distinguished place in the convent. Chalabi Efendi, at the same time, is the Imâm, Mesnewihan and member of the Mawlâna Convent. If someone else is appointed for performing the duty of Mesnewihan, the place of Mesnewihan during the semâ performance will be next to the Tarîkatçi Dede. Ser-tarîk is responsible for dedes in the convent, ser-tabbâh is responsible for suffering souls. Besides these, there are some officials like charity clerk (vakıf kâtibi), doorman (bevvâb), librarian (kütüphaneci). The positions of Tarîkatçilik, guards Shams and Âteshbaz is only confined to Konya; there is not any in the other cities. As the position of matbah-ı şerif (head of the cook) is not available in Zâviyes (small dervish lodges) there is not any employees regarding here.

In an âsitane there are dervishes (dedes) who had the experienced of one thousand and one days suffering and suffering souls who are still sufferings. Dedes stay in a small room, which is called hücre (cell), one or two and three people at one time; souls (can) stay in the kitchen. Dervishes those who are experiencing sufferings, if they want, are able to stay in the convent as a single, take salary from convent's income; or stay outside, find a job, get married and come and go.

Besides these people, there are followers (muhib) those who are coming and going, participating activities. (Muhib is someone who is joined to the tarîqat, blessed by the sheikh, however, this term is usually used for those who are connected to the Mawlawî sect but had not have the experience of chille -forty days suffering-). Those whom generation go back to Chalabis, accepting salary from the charity, must follow the customs and controls of the convent in Konya and they participate the activities in here.

We can summarize the principle of spiritual education in Mawlawí order as follows: 1. To obtain the basic and the necessary knowledge regarding Sufism and the Religion, 2. Obeying the religious obligations and the Sunna of the Prophet, 3. to learn submission, discipline, obedience and service, 4. To learn the manner of the principle of Taríqat, politeness, semâ, chatting, course, lesson, etc. 5. To develop himself reading the main works of the tariqat such as Mathnawí, Minhâcü'l-fuqarâ, Menâqıb etc. 6. Self education through practicing eating less, sleeping less, speaking less; keeping clean the heart; to have the manner of being good suspicious, 7. Attending the dhikr (remembrance) of glory names, keeping busy with evrâd u ezkâr 8. To receive inspirations from saints and always keeping himself in a condition of self-inspection, 9. With these all, try to obtain using the principle of mevt-i irâdî, the elixir of love. Besides this should make himself busy with sâzendelik, hânendelik, poetry, calligraphy, handcrafts which will be useful in mukâbele-i şerif or special times or places.

As it is known that music has a special meaning in the world of Mawlawí order. Mawlâna begins his Mathnawí with the reed (nay) story and he speaks through the mouth of it. He expresses the special moment like this: "Hence philosophers have said that we received these harmonies from the revolution of the (celestial) sphere, (And that) this (melody) which people sing with pandore (tanbúr) and throat is the sound of the revolutions of the sphere; (But) the true believers say that the influences of Paradise made every unpleasant sound to be beautiful. We all have been parts of Adam, we have heard those melodies in Paradise. Although the water and earth (of our bodies) have caused a doubt to fall upon us, something of those (melodies) comes (back) to our memory; But since it is mingled with the earth of sorrow, how should this treble and bass give (us) the same delight? Therefore semá (music) is the food of lovers (of God), since therein is the phantasy of composure (tranquillity of mind)."

The semâ, which is a ritual form of Mawlawís, every part, movements and dress in semâ have special symbolic meanings. For example, camel's hair hat (sikke) represents the tombstone of the ego; his cardigan (hırka) represents the ego's tomb; his white skirt represents the ego's shroud. At the beginning of the Semâ, by holding his arms crosswise, the semâzen appears to represent the number one, thus testifying to God's unity. While whirling, his arms are open: his right arm is directed to the sky, ready to receive God's beneficence; his left hand, upon which his eyes are fastened, is turned toward the earth. The semâzen conveys God's spiritual gift to those who are witnessing the Semâ. The Semâ ceremony represents the human being's spiritual journey, an ascent by means of intelligence and love to Perfection (Kemâl). Turning toward the truth, he grows through love, transcends the ego, meets the truth, and arrives at Perfection. We have testified from sources that semâ, as a form of ceremony before Mawlâna, was performed by many taríqats. However, after his choosing it, the semâ as a component is getting increased its attraction more and more for both foreign and local people for centuries even today.

In our opinion, the most important examples of display arts and elegance lessons in our society is available in the Mawlawí order and semâ ceremony (mukâbele-i şerîfe). The ceremony, with its elegance and magnificence, is consisting of all body movement in a perfect consistency and a harmony with accompaniment of sound, voice and music. These perfect movements and conducts surround life of a Mawlawí derwish. The main factor, which provides disciplines, is absolute obedience and attributing holiness to existences and objects and behaving in a good manner. Actually, good examples of elegance, good manners and delicate jokes of word, movement and manners can be possible to see in Mawlâna's epics. Reflecting elegance and dignity outside is one of the principles of the taríqat, either during the ceremony (âyin) and worshiping, or somewhere crying loudly, shouting, tearing off collar etc. is considered inappropriate.

Consequently, Mawlawí sect, which was formed as a systematised taríqat by a great thinker and a Sùfí Mawlâna Jalâleddîn-i Rûmî's son Sultan Walad through inspiration of his father's thoughts and ideas, is known as the way of love, eagerness, semâ and safâ; its followers served with their good manners, elegances, delicate souls, artistry to our society for centuries.

REMEMBRANCES AND ADVICES FROM MAWLÂNA

The following remembrances, notes and words are usually collected from the first period of Seljuki sources that are related to Mawlâna. The most significant works in question are Sultan Walad's Ibtidânâme, Sipehsâlâr's Risâle and Ahmed Eflâkî's Menâkıbü'l-Ârifîn.

AFTER THE DEATH OF MAWLÂNA:

Due to Mawlâna's will, Shaykhulislâm Sadreddîn-i Konevî who would have people prayed for Mawlâna, however, when he about to begin praying, lost his conscious, then Qadı Sirajeddîn-i Urmewî who was a scholar of its time, had let the pray. Not only the Muslim inhabitants of Konya but also all the followers of other religions attended Mawlâna's funeral. The funeral was became very crowded. People were shouting and feeling faint, bursting into tears. For a moment, Muslims wanted to make them go away because of crowd. Then the followers of the other religion said to Muslim: "we understood the realities of Moses, Jesus and the other prophets from his clear words and saw in him the nature and behaviour of the mature prophets that we had read in our books. If you are his friend, we are his friend, too. He said that 72 nations listened to their secret from them and that they were a flute that gave hundreds of sounds out of a screen. Mawlâna's body is the sun of realities that shines on people and gives them favour. All of the world likes sun. All houses are being lightened by its light. Mawlâna is like bread. Nobody can say that he does not need bread. Is there any hungry person who runs away from bread?"

MAWLÂNA'S TOMB: Mawlâna's body was buried in Gülbahçe (Rosegarden), which was given as a gift to Bahâeddin Walad by Sultan Alaaddín Keykubat, that is known now as the Tomb of Mawlâna where is located in his father's head side.

MAWLÂNA JALÂLEDDÎN-I RÛMÎ

The tomb which is called now Kubbe-i Hadrâ (Green Dome), with the effort of Sultan Walad and Alâmeddin Kayser who is a statesman and endless support of Gürcü Hatun, wife of powerful Seljuk vizier Muîneddin Süleyman Pervâne who is know with his loyalty to Mawlâna, was commissioned in 1274. its architect was Badreddîn-i Tebrîzî. Mawlâna's family members, close friends and Chalabies from his lineage were buried here. The side domes which are located in the right and left sides of the green dome, were built at the time of Karamanoğlu Alâeddin Ali Bey in 14th and 15th century. Semâhane (Ritual Dance Hall) at the north side of this section and mosque, Dervish cells around the courtyard and tombs were added in Ottoman period in 16th century. With the combination of the maydân-ı sharîf (large assembly chamber), matbah-ı sheriff (kitchen), shadırvan (fountain), the pool of shab-i ârûs (nuptial night), the dervish convent became a complex of building.

After the 4th September 1925, a law was passed closing all the "Tekkes' (dervish loges) and "Zawiyes' (small dervish lodges), Mawlawí taríqat became history; however, two years later in 1927, Konya Mawlâna Mausoleum was allowed to reopen as a Museum for the visitors. The activities started in 1940 as gatherings of remembrance of Mawlâna, later it is became celebration. With the cooperation of Governance of Konya, Metropolitan Municipality of Konya and the University of Selcuk, several festivals and semâ âyins (whirling rituals) were held in every May and December of the year. It lasts two weeks and its culminating point is the 17th December called Shab-i Arus meaning "Nuptial Night", the night of Wedding.

The Mawlâna museum is the most second visited historical place in Turkey after the Topkapı Saray Museum. It appears wit its magnificent dome, spacious places, majestic tomb, internal design which deeply surrounds the person and excites visitors. Among the increasing amount of the visitors ever year, foreign tourists who are coming from around the world constitutes highly important total.

DID MAWLÂNA'S FATHER RAISE HIMSELF UPRIGHT WHEN HIS BODY WAS BROUGHT?

When Mawlâna departed towards God, he was buried head side of his father, Sultânu'l-Ulemâ Bahâeddín Walad, after that a tomb was built here. Over the grave of Mawlâna, one of the carving Selcuki art marvellous wooden sarcophagus was made by an artist called Abdülvâhid. The sarcophagus covered Mawlâna's grave remained for many years, until the 16th century, Kanuni Sultan Süleyman had a marble sarcophagus made to cover the grave of Mawlâna and that of his son Sultan Walad buried beside him. This was covered with gold worked cloths, and the wooden sarcophagus placed over the grave of Mawlâna's father Bahâeddin Walad. The height of this wooden sarcophagus gives it the appearance of having been stoop up at the end, giving rise to a story that "when Mawlâna's body was brought here for burial his father raised himself upright" on account of the respect he felt for his son's wisdom. People interpreted it because of its majestic view.

"LET OUR DISCIPLES BUILD A HIGH TOMB"

One day pír Mawlâna had uttered ""Let our disciples build a high tomb which can be seen from far and wide. If any one sees our tomb from a far distance, and believes and has confidence in our sainthood, God will put him or her among those who receive divine mercy. Especially, if he or her who visits, and prays at our tomb with full of love and sincere faith free of hypocrisy, sincere truth free of metaphor, and true knowledge free of suspicion, God will fulfill his every need and make him attain his wishes. His all religious and worldly wishes will turn out to be true."

"THIS CITY WILL BE PROTECTED TILL THE RESURRECTION DAY"

The Mongolian commander Bayju, when he surrounded Konya by a great army, people of Konya requested from Mawlâna to pray, he had said as follows "Do not worry! The Great Allah donated you to Shaykh Salâhaddin. This city will be protected from Mongolian's swords. Whoever attacks to Konya, will never escape from our stroke. As long as the holy body of Bahâheddin Walad Hazrat is buried here, by the Will of God, this city will be remained safe from all kinds of calamities; this city will have a great fame in the world and those who will replace my post will remain in here on the condition of healthiness and safeness."

"YOU TOO DO NOT UNDERSTAND OF THIS!"

One day Mawlâna was sitting beside the pool at the garden reading a book. At that moment, Shams approached him asking what you are reading. Mawlâna "You do not understand of these" he said. Then Shams Tabrízí starts to throw the books into the pool. Mawlâna was in a slight flurry, he expressed his worries with saying: "What a pity was to my father's valuable books". When Shams saw his sorrows, after a short while, he extends his arm and takes the books out of the pool and gave them to Mawlâna. He was surprised and when he saw that the inks of any books seem unruined and did not get wet, "How can it be possible? he asked. Then Shams-i Tabrízí said "It is a secret; you too do not understand of this".

REASON OF HIS COMING TO THE ASSEMBLY: Mawlâna was always attending the latest when he was sure that all the followers of him approached the talk gatherings and semâ assemblies at the palace of statesmen. Husâmeddín Chalabi asked him regarding his wondering about this attitude. Mawlâna said to him: "If we enter the palace fist, the guardians might stop entering some of our friends who come after me. They then can not attend our meeting. If we are not able to enter them into a vazier's or an emír's door in this world, how can I enter them tomorrow into the hereafter palace and presence of Allah?

"IF YOU DO NOT HAVE LESSON FROM ALLAH AND HIS PROPHET'S WORDS..." One day a great statesman, Muîneddin Pervane, came to visit Mawlâna whom sincerely devoted himself asking to give advice. After thinking a while in his head bent, he raised his head and said to Muîneddin Pervane: "O Commander Muîneddin! I heard that you are memorising Qur'an is that right? Muîneddin was in a happy situation "yes" said he. Mawlâna again, "You are listening to Jâmlü'l-Usûl from Shaykh Sadreddín". Pervane confirmed it. Thereupon, Mawlâna said: "Since you are not having lessons from Allah and his Prophet's words, will you have lesson from my words." Muîneddin Pervane was ashamed and left presence crying.

"IF YOU WANT YOUR ENEMY WANTS TO LOVE YOU..." Mawlâna, one day, while chatting with his son Sultan Walad said him: "O Bahaeddin! If you want to love your enemy and want your enemy loves you; tell his goodness and kindness for forty days. When the day come that enemy becomes your friend because there is a way from heart to tongue and from tongue to heart."

"WAIT ME TOO!" Mawlâna was passing through a district, the children who are playing in the street run into him wanted to kiss his hand when they saw him. A boy who was just the beginning of the game he called out saying "wait me too, I am coming too"; however he forgot it and continued his game. Mawlâna with a great humility and a self-sacrificing waited the child without being sicken of and being fed up. At the end, the child who was satisfied came to kiss Mawlâna's hand.

"WE HAVE EXCEEDED PRIEST IN HUMILITY" One day couple of priests those who came to visit Mawlâna, meet them on the way and respectfully they bow their heads. Mawlâna responded to their attitudes with the same way they did. When the priests raised their heads, Mawlâna's head still was the same respect position and this greetings repeated couple of times. When Mawlâna returned to Madrasah said to Sultan Walad: "Thanks Allah! today we did not leave humility to priests."

"I ACCEPTED THEM AS TO BE MY FOLLOWER BECAUSE THEY ARE BAD" at the speech of Muîneddin Pervane in his gathering in a divan at the palace: "Mawlâna is a man who hardly grown up for centuries. There is not a Sultan like him. However those who are around him are bad people" uttered he. Someone who was in the gathering conveyed this word to Mawlâna. Mawlâna wrote Muîneddin a letter saying "If they were good, I would be a follower for them; I accepted them as my follower because they are bad."

"COME, COME AGAIN WHOEVER YOU ARE, COME!" wonderer, fire worshipper or idolatrous, come! Come even if you broke your penitence a hundred times, Ours is the portal of hope, come as you are." Mawlâna's famous rubâî which is considered the most universal message, is found only at the end of one copy manuscript of Dîvân-ı Kebîr; we do not have enough evidence that it is belongs to Mawlâna. Mawlâna uttered many couplets starting with "Come, come" or "let's come, let's come" and he had said very often-

promising hope words, the rubâî might be attributed him. However, so called rubâî, is found in the founder of Khorasan Sufi movement Ebû Saîd-i Ebu'l-Hayr's published poems. Therefore, it should not be contradictory to Mawlâna's thought world. These words, like this comment "irrespective of religion and faith, considering all human beings are one". For my view, such a thinker who spent all his life for the sake of the love of Allah and the love the Prophet and for sufferings, barely he based his idea of respect to human being and tolerance on these two phenomena, can not be appropriated with his way of thinking.

MAWLÂNA'S WILL: Mawlâna had left to those who are around him: "I advice you to fear of Allah whether secretly and openly, eat less, sleep less, speak less. Avoiding from sins, keep fasting and praying ritual prays, always be aware of self desires, bearing sufferings of people, meeting with spiritually high quality and good people and keep being away from vulgar people. The best of people is to be beneficial for people. The best of the word is less and meaning the aim. Praise is confined to Allah alone. Greetings to the people of Tawhíd (monotheism).

SEVEN ADVICES: The seven advices of Mawlâna are as follow:

In generosity and helping others, be like a river.

In compassion and grace be like the sun.

In concealing others' faults be like the night.

In anger and fury be like one who is dead.

In modesty and humility be like the earth.

In tolerance be like a sea.

Either exist as you are, or be as you look!

MAWLÂNA JALÂLEDDÎN-I RÛMÎ

BIBLIOGRAPHY: (I am providing some books, which give general and specific information about the life of Mawlâna and his works, thoughts, history of Mawlawí and its manner): A. Selâhaddin Hidayetoğlu, "Hazret-i Mevlâna Muhammed Celâleddin-i Rûmî", Konya, 1996. Abdülbaki Gölpınarlı, "Mevlâna Celâleddin", 4th edt., Ist., 1985. Abdülbaki Gölpınarlı, "Mevlâna'dan Sonra Mevlevîlik", 2nd edt., Ist., 1982. Adnan Karaismailoğlu, "Mevlâna ve Mesnevi", Ankara, 2001. Ahmet Kabaklı, "Mevlâna", Ist., 1972. Ali Nihad Tarlan, "Mevlâna", Ist., 1974. Bedîuzzaman Furûzanfer, "Mevlâna Celâleddin", translated by F.Nafiz Uzluk, Ist., 1963. Celâlettin Çelebi, "Hazret-i Mevlâna", Konya, 1997. Cihan Okuyucu, "İçimizdeki Mevlâna", Ist., 2002. Emine Yeniterzi, "Mevlâna Celâleddin Rûmî", Ankara, 1995. Feyzi Halıcı, "Mevlâna Celâleddin", Konya, 1982. H.Hüseyin Top, "Mevlevî Usûl ve Adabı", Ist., 200. Hasan Özönder, "Konya Mevlâna Dergâhı", Ankara, 1989. İsmail Yakıt, "Batı Düşüncesi ve Mevlâna", Ist., 2000. İsmet Kayaoğlu, "Mevlâna ve Mevlevilik", Konya, 2002. Mehmet Önder, "Mevlâna ve Mevlevîlik", Ist., 1998. Mustafa Uslu, "Mevlâna", Ist., 2004. Sezai Küçük, "Mevlevîliğin Son Yüzyılı", Ist., 2003. Şefik Can, "Mevlâna Hayatı, Şahsiyeti, Fikirleri", Ist., 1995. Yakup Şafak, "Mevlâna Celâleddin Rûmî Bütün Eserleri-Seçmeler", Konya, 2004. (Note: Sample couplets which were quoted from Mathnawí see R. Nicholson edition and V. Izbudak translations; for the gazels in Divan-ı Kebir see: A. Golpınarlı published by Minister of Culture and Tourism; the rubâís were quoted and got benefited from N. Gencosman's works and the numbers were given according to these works.)